Facilitator's Guide

10 STEPS TO

Be a Successful Manager

Lisa Haneberg

ASTD
PRESS

Alexandria, Virginia

ASTD Press is an internationally renowned source of insightful and practical information on workplace learning and performance topics, including training basics, evaluation and return-on-investment (ROI), instructional systems development (ISD), e-learning, leadership, and career development.

Ordering information: Books published by ASTD Press can be purchased by visiting our website at store.astd.org or by calling 800.628.2783 or 703.683.8100.

Library of Congress Control Number: 2007921482
ISBN-10: 1-56286-476-9
ISBN-13: 978-1-56286-476-7

ASTD Press Editorial Staff
Director: Cat Russo
Manager, Acquisitions & Author Relations: Mark Morrow
Editorial Manager: Jacqueline Edlund-Braun
Editorial Assistant: Maureen Soyars

Copyeditor: Christine Cotting
Proofreader: Kris Patenaude
Interior Design and Production: UpperCase Publication Services, Ltd.
Cover Design: Renita Wade

Printed by Victor Graphics, Inc., Baltimore, Maryland, www.victorgraphics.com

C O N T E N T S

Being a management trainer is an honor and a challenge. We have the opportunity and privilege to affect how our companies are led and managed. We can help define and reinforce the desired work climate through our work with managers. Great managers make great companies. But great managers are not born, and management can't be learned in one weeklong course. I've been training and coaching managers for more than 25 years and I can't imagine a better way to make a living.

Great management trainers also are not born that way. We must develop and expand skills and try new learning models to meet ever-changing business goals and challenges. I created this *Facilitator's Guide* to accompany my book, *10 Steps to Be a Successful Manager,* to provide and spark ideas for making management training respond to these changing needs. The *Guide* is written in an informal style—much like a conversation—to engage you in the ways you can use this book to strengthen your management team's skills.

I've been both a manager and a management trainer and I know that both jobs are demanding and important. Time is precious and our to-do lists are long. I hope you find this *Facilitator's Guide* for *10 Steps to Be a Successful Manager* helpful and easy to use. Managers are the engines for corporate success and we—management trainers—are the master mechanics who can help tune up and repair the function.

I would love to hear how you are using this guide. Please feel free to drop me an email with your stories and questions. I can be reached through my website at www.lisahaneberg.com.

Lisa Haneberg
October 2007

The Opportunity to Improve Management Capacity

As a management development training professional, I've attended or used many of the best-known training programs: Covey, Achieve Global, DDI, Tom Peters, Center for Creative Leadership, Linkage, and many other programs from smaller companies. Those programs are great and have value. Nonetheless, I feel there's something missing with regard to the training I want to provide managers.

I believe management is a craft. It's a practice that builds over time and should improve with experience. The magic word there is *should*, right? Some managers get better and some don't. In my experience, there are a few reasons some managers don't build their craft:

◆ They don't have good role models or informal coaches to steer and influence their development.

- Their development has been punctuated by several training events (many being flavor-of-the-month programs) rather than consistent growth. These managers learn to wait a month before making any changes because there's a good chance the program will be forgotten or replaced by some other trendy approach.

- Organization leaders and trainers (that's us) expect far too little from managers—so

POINTER

Catalyst

A catalyst is a substance that increases the rate of a chemical reaction but is not consumed in the process. The catalyst generally is used in much smaller amounts than the other chemicals in the reaction. Some of the most common catalysts in everyday life are the platinum, rhodium, and palladium in the catalytic converters on automobiles. Very small amounts of these rare and expensive metals speed the conversion of dangerous nitrogen oxides and carbon monoxide into less harmful compounds.

In business, the term *catalyst* has come to describe a person who activates, accelerates, or otherwise increases the rate of reaction to a situation. It's someone who, through proactive dialogue or action, causes an important (and presumably beneficial) event to occur. Catalysts can trigger negative events, too, but that's not the kind of catalyst I suggest being. We can add a lot of value by being a positive catalyst.

that's what we get. I've seen few organizations in which professional management is expected and developed.

◆ We aren't tapping into our managers' intrinsic motivations to be amazing performers.

As a fellow trainer, I would guess you've observed these same situations. You know that managers *can* make a significant contribution to the organization, but often they don't. This challenge is a huge opportunity for us. Managers are the engines of the organization. Their health and effectiveness determine the health and effectiveness of the organization. If we can influence and affect the managers, we can influence and affect the entire system.

Management development trainers have the opportunity to be catalysts for organizational excellence. Our potential impact is huge. When managers perform at their peak, the organization hums and people enjoy their work. Conversely, poor management damages every aspect of the work environment. Why do people leave your company? Many people don't leave *jobs*—they leave bad managers.

We're the catalysts for managerial excellence, and being a management trainer can be the most important and rewarding work we'll ever do. Really, it's that cool. And it's why I do what I do. I love catalyzing management breakthroughs—big ones and teeny-tiny ones.

Catalysts—you'll see this term throughout the *Facilitator's Guide*. I recommend you approach using *10 Steps to Be a Successful Manager* as catalytic development—training that, on the surface, offers solid techniques but, more deeply, also produces powerful shifts in thinking and assumptions. I'll tell you more about the design and intent of the book in chapter 3. For now, just know that I've sprinkled a little magic catalytic dust in each part of this book.

They say you can take the trainer out of the classroom, but you can't get the trainer out of the writing. OK, nobody said that, but it's true in my case. As a trainer, I had to write *10 Steps to Be a Successful Manager* from a development perspective and with its use as a training tool in mind. Here are the questions I tried to answer when writing that book:

◆ What gets in the way of middle success?

◆ What have I seen or done that's worked to develop management capacity?

◆ What could I offer in a book that would most benefit readers?

◆ How can I do that in a way that's highly catalytic?

The techniques and practices offered in *10 Steps to Be a Successful Manager* can benefit managers at all levels of the organization and all levels of experience. Management has been given a bad rap over the years—as excess overhead and waste—but that's inaccurate because great managers are worth their weight in gold.

The goal of this *Facilitator's Guide* is to offer trainers, coaches, and other learning professionals guidance on creating great manager training using the book *10 Steps to Be a Successful Manager.* Rather than presenting a more traditional guide with a play-by-play set of facilitation instructions, I've chosen to give you the framework for great manager training, along with suggested agendas. The idea is that, from this logical framework, you'll be able to create meaningful conversations about effective management among members of your team, group, or division, and even on an individual level. How you choose to use this guidebook depends on your individual circumstances.

To assist in this development, I've included lots of space for you to take notes and capture ideas as you read through the book. Gather these notes and ideas, and create your own effective learning sessions based on the principles in the *10 Steps* companion book. Here's a quick tour of what this book offers you.

The Roadmap

◆ **Chapter 1:** In this chapter you'll find the 10 components that enhance learning and application for any training participant.

- **Chapter 2:** Here you'll find specific details about management training, including the competencies and experience a good management trainer should possess.

- **Chapter 3:** This chapter offers you notes on each of the 10 manager training steps offered in *10 Steps to be a Successful Manager,* along with discussion topics (ideas to generate lively conversations) and activity suggestions (ideas to get participants to explore and try the step techniques).

- **Chapter 4:** One of the most effective training methods is informal learning. This chapter offers my favorite informal training ideas, with suggestions on how to apply them to the *10 Steps* book.

- **Chapter 5:** Here are sample training agendas that enable you to take your ideas and create your own training program based on what works best for your managers, including one-day, two-day, and one-week agendas.

- **Chapter 6:** To help you quickly create training, I provide full-size reproducible versions of each example, table, tool, and worksheet used in *10 Steps to Be a Successful Manager* (the electronic versions are included as printable .pdf files on the companion CD-ROM).

Thanks for coming along on this journey with me to catalyze managerial excellence, and I wish you great success using the book to enhance your management development programs. I'd love to hear from you. If you have any questions or comments, or if you'd like to share your stories, send me an email. You can find my email address and links to my work at my website, www.lisahaneberg.com.

Management Training Success: 10 Components

As I get older and wiser (one hopes), I become more and more convinced that training needs to be as natural and uncontrolled as possible. That's right, *uncontrolled*—the less I try to control the training, the better it is. As a longtime recovering control freak (I love to control things!), this has been a difficult journey for me. But *not* trying to control training is a wonderful effort. It takes some courage and confidence, but it always leads to a better outcome. That's also the case when managing meetings and projects.

The most effective learning sessions are not polished, practiced, or choreographed ahead of time. The best training sets the stage for something to happen—and then lets things happen.

This *Facilitator's Guide* reflects these thoughts and doesn't offer scripts or minute-by-minute facilitation instructions. I don't want to present this material in a glossy way because I don't think this approach will encourage you to apply the techniques.

You might call this the "salon approach to training," and I think it's the right method for management and leadership development programs. Salons are organic, stimulating, and transformative. Comments become catalysts that change how people approach their work.

10 Factors That Enhance Learning and Application

Here's my top-10 list of the factors that improve the application and habituation of learning:

1. sound science

2. star power

3. trainer magnetism

4. provocation

5. evocation

6. connecting conversation

7. diversity of thought

8. depth versus breadth

9. relevance

10. tactile trying.

Sound Science

Training needs to be built on a solid foundation. The techniques must work. The theories ought to make sense. That may seem elemental and obvious, but I've attended training programs that were way off the weird scale. Managers don't have time for such mumbo-jumbo—they need real-life concepts and practices that will help them get their jobs done today. Challenging the status quo is wonderful, but introducing something for the sake of being fun or intellectually stimulating is a waste of time and resources.

Star Power

Let's face it: Famous people sell their concepts well. If your managers can see Marcus Buckingham, Tom Peters, or Benjamin Zander in person (or on DVD), the message has star power.

What does this mean for you? Don't be hesitant to get a famous face to say what you want to say. Open your training with an inspiring DVD or ask participants to read an article from the *Harvard Business Review* as course pre-work. Many famous people are saying the same things we are—use them!

One caution: Resist latching onto gimmicks, acronyms, or flavor-of-the-month-type stuff. Our managers have become very wary of this time-dated material, and rightly so.

Trainer Magnetism

Are you a magnetic trainer? These are people whom others like to hang around at work. They're magnetic because people enjoy talking with them for some reason—maybe they're fun, interesting, great listeners, or super smart. We all have qualities that help draw people toward us, and we need to use those qualities. If people like being with you, they'll come to more training sessions and they'll participate more fully. Both introverts and extrovert can be magnetic trainers. Being an awesome listener is likely a common trait most magnetic trainers share. (I've written more about how to listen in chapter 2 of this guide).

Provocation

Learning often occurs as a result of dissonance, or some difference between what we thought was so and another perspective. When our training is provocative, it challenges participants to think in new ways. We shouldn't endeavor to be provocative for its own sake. We need to notice where participants are getting stuck and then offer development that nudges them forward. Something is provocative when it causes a strong reaction—for example, all of these reactions may be provoked: annoyance, anger, excitement, fascination, and curiosity. Although we don't want to anger our training participants routinely, an occasional bit of anger or frustration, followed by deep conversation, can be a great learning enhancer.

Evocation

When we're evocative, we help others see things from their perspective—we put people in the scene for themselves. Evocative learning is very connective. When you see people think about a concept, or when they apply it to their situation, their thoughts are being evoked. Great training provokes evocation. We want managers to be imagining how they will apply the concepts or techniques in their departments.

Connecting Conversation

Connecting conversation is dialogue that brings concepts, people, and things together. Trainers need to help make connections between what's being discussed in a training class and real-world business opportunities and challenges. Have you noticed how lively and engaging conversations become when lots of people jump in and share their unique perspectives? Connecting conversation draws participation because it's interesting, helpful, and mentally stimulating.

Diversity of Thought

I love putting together training groups filled with people who seem to share nothing in common. Oh, what fun it is to bring these diverse perspectives together on one topic. Everyone learns more, and the conversations will be both evocative and provocative. I also like bringing in diverse expert opinions by having participants read articles with opposing viewpoints for pre-work. Diversity is not just interesting and healthy; it's necessary for managers to make good decisions. The training environment is a perfect place to help build managers' appreciation for diverse thoughts, opinions, and approaches.

Depth versus Breadth

As you'll notice throughout this guide, I prefer to address fewer training topics for more time. The deeper you can get into a topic, the deeper the learning will be. Trainers often make the mistake of acquiescing to managers who say they don't have time for training. We pack 12 topics in a one-day training session, knowing all the while that it's not going to lead to a good result. Great training goes deep—it takes some time with the concepts and techniques so that managers can make the connection to their work and realize the training's relevance.

Relevance

Great training meets a need. It gets something done. It does a job. When managers need help, there's a job to be done. Training might be the answer to help fill that need (although it's not always the answer, of course). Our training needs to serve managers, employees, and the organization. If we can't identify the job we want our training to do, we ought to question whether it's the right training at the right time.

Tactile Trying

Great training invites people to touch it, feel it, and give it a try. Training ought to be a laboratory for safely testing thoughts and techniques. You'll notice that most of the exercises I recommend in this *Facilitator's Guide* are based on real-life job tasks and challenges. The best training engages people in working with the material. We should encourage our participants to take the training apart, then put it back together in whatever way works best for them—like a car buff would do to better understand how the engine works.

◆ ◆ ◆

There you have them, my 10 factors that enhance learning and application. Think about the next training session you plan to facilitate and how you might be able to strengthen some of these factors for that session. The changes required to help a session go from flat to engaging, from boring to provocative, from abstract to concrete are often very small.

CHAPTER TWO

Management Training Skills

By now you've picked up that I care a great deal about how we train managers. As the engines for our organizations, they deserve effective development that doesn't waste their precious time.

Being a management trainer is important and rewarding work, and I applaud you for dedicating your time and energy to that endeavor. To be sure, it's not the career for everyone. When we hit a grand-slam home run in our training, we make a significant contribution to the organization. When we fail to deliver value for the time and resources we spend (ours and our learners'), we lose an important opportunity.

What does it take to be a great management trainer? I could create a list of 15 skills I think all trainers ought to have, but I don't think that would serve you well. You've heard of the 80/20 rule, right? The 80/20 rule states that the top 20 percent will produce 80 percent of the results. I think the 80/20 rule applies well to management training.

The 20 Percent That Will Get You 80 Percent

There are four characteristics or skills that I believe are most vital for effective management trainers—they constitute the short list (20 percent) and make the greatest difference to results (80 percent). I might cause a stir by suggesting these are the *top* four, but here goes:

1. previous successful experience as a manager

2. business acumen

3. passion and talent for being a catalyst

4. ability to create and facilitate great dialogue.

Previous Successful Experience as a Manager

I'll start off by discussing the most controversial point on that short list of traits. Do management trainers need to have management experience? I think they do, and I think they need to have been *great managers*. Management is a tough job; and to help managers learn and grow, I think it's necessary to have done the work. For a management trainer to garner trust, confidence, and influence with managers, she or he needs to be able to relate to managers from a position of common ground.

Remember, I also suggest that management training ought not be formal or rehearsed. If trainers could memorize the content and present it, then management experience wouldn't be needed. At the foundation of the best management training is creating great business discussions, and I believe that the best people to facilitate those discussions are trainers who've done management work.

I know this notion may not be popular because there are thousands of management trainers who have never managed. Here's my advice for those of you who are management trainers without management experience—get management experience. Volunteer to be on the board of your local ASTD chapter (be president). Ask to lead complex projects. As part of your development, take two years to work as supervisor or department manager.

And one more thought that might not be popular: If taking on the role of manager for two years (or more) doesn't sound pleasant to you, then I would question whether you ought to be a management trainer. I think management trainers should love management, and they should enjoy being a manager. How will you be a powerful catalyst for managers if you find their jobs unappealing? If you don't want to be a manager, that will come through in your training work.

The old saying goes something like this: Those who can't do, teach. Bunk! If you can't manage, and you don't want to learn to manage well, don't try training managers. I would recruit management trainers from the management ranks—recruit the very best and help them see the amazing contribution they could make by helping other managers excel.

Business Acumen

Management development is the art of helping managers manage a *business*. Everything about the training we provide to managers is about business. We help them understand their business and we help them choose and develop practices that enable them to run their pieces of the business. Business, business, business. To be an effective management trainer, you need to know business.

The term *business acumen* means knowledge of how the business runs so that we can make good judgments and decisions. It's important that we're aware of our company's key indicators, its strategies, its target customers, and its market position. We ought to understand the key processes that managers use to run the business—budgeting, goal setting, forecasting, financial analysis, project implementation, hiring, and others.

Here's the good news: If you've had successful management experience, you likely already possess business acumen. Management trainers without direct management experience need to ensure they understand the business before attempting to train managers. If you don't understand the business, it will be difficult to facilitate catalyzing conversations, and your lack of skill will stand out like a double-breasted suit at a Jimmy Buffett concert.

Passion and Talent for Being a Catalyst

The first two characteristics focus on background—the skills and experiences that will help you influence and develop managers. This third characteristic is all about heart and motivation.

I think it's critical that we're driven to catalyze growth and development. It's not easy work and will require you to demonstrate assertiveness, courage, and a deep reverence for the craft of management. Perhaps you think I'm being a bit dramatic. OK, I'll admit that I'm on the high side of passion for management development—and here's why: I've seen a lot of management training that made no difference (or made a negative difference), and seeing such waste drives me crazy. I'm not being righteous. Earlier in my career, I delivered management training that I now see was not a good use of the time, energy, and resources devoted to it. I don't ever want to do that again, and I hope nothing but success for you.

Every management trainer I've met has been smart, hard-working, and well meaning—every one of them. If we're going to pour ourselves into our work, let's make it count. Let's be catalysts for management transformation!

What does it take to be a catalyst? In the following paragraphs, I'm going to describe several "ways of being" that can be catalytic. The bottom line is to be more in tune with what's needed for each situation—to do that which will best enable the transformation. Honing my abilities to be a catalyst is a lifelong pursuit of mine, and I'd love nothing more than to help you develop your catalyst's muscles as well.

It's tough to be a catalyst if you are not proactive. *Being proactive* is the first way of being for training catalysts. Listen and respond to what people are saying—and to what they obviously are not saying. Challenge managers—intellectually and with regard to their intrinsic motivation—by stepping the conversation up to the next level of intimacy, complexity, or controversy. Take the initiative to offer learning solutions for today's business problems. Don't take months to support today's need. Offer now the training that's needed now. Take the initiative to get the right people together in conversation. Do whatever it takes to get people involved in the learning process.

The second way of being for catalysts is to *be curious*. Catalysts often are naturally curious people (trainers, too, right?). The more you encourage your curiosity, the more likely that you'll be able to catalyze transformation. I see a strong connection between curiosity and learning because learning happens in layers. The outer layer is the surface and that's the kind of learning that occurs in any training session. As we go deeper, learning becomes much more personal and connective—connecting to work, interests, problems, and passions. Curiosity is often the vehicle we use to go deeper. We keep hiking because we're curious about what's around the next bend. We keep listening because we're curious about where the conversation is heading. We ask more questions because we're curious about what someone will say. Let your curiosity flourish. Ask open-ended questions about what things mean and how they operate. Take an interest in understanding why and how things work.

This next way of being is the one I see the least—*be courageous*. Great trainers are very courageous people. We have to be brave because that's how we make the greatest difference. This is where we can and should lead. Courage plays a big part in creating great dialogue because it's often what's not being said that needs to be said. Do you let training discussions ride on the surface, or do you ask that one question—the tough question—that turns the conversation upside down and gets everyone nervously engaged? I've never known of a situation in which a trainer was fired for being courageous. Having courage is not really risky, but you may find it uncomfortable or scary. Tension isn't always a bad thing; it means that people are thinking and feeling. As long as you can get the conversation moving forward, putting a little tension in the room by bringing up what's on everyone's mind and no one's lips can be a great catalyst. Help training participants be more inclusive and authentic.

The final important way of being is to *be observant*. To be a great catalyst, you have to notice what's going on. Keep up with what's happening in the business and in each department. In your training sessions, notice the topics and behaviors (and perhaps the people) that seem to engage or disengage participants. Notice the major obstacles within the organization and enable your training to help obliterate managers' productivity barriers. Share your observations in ways that stimulate input and participation.

It's fun to be a positive catalyst. Most of us get into the field of training because we like to see the lightbulbs come on over people's heads when they have that aha moment. Catalysts create those moments every day.

Ability to Create and Facilitate Great Dialogue

Trainers need to generate and facilitate great business conversations. I wrote about the importance of this skill as it relates to coaching in chapter 4 of *Coaching Basics* (ASTD Press 2006). The point is the same for coaching and for training—we need to inspire and catalyze great conversation. Here's the coaching discussion adapted for trainers.

Good conversation should be exciting, fast-paced, and intellectually stimulating. Everyone is smart and focused. People solve problems quickly and think on their feet. Do you wish you could experience such a provocative work environment? Some workplaces are like this and, more often than not, the reason is that they hire the right people and foster productive and engaging dialogue. People are talking about topics that matter, and what they talk about matters to them.

Painters need to understand the nature and properties of oils and canvas. English teachers need to know semicolons and dangling participles. Training occurs in conversation, so trainers need to be master conversationalists. As a trainer, you have the opportunity to create great dialogue and help managers become master conversationalists. When your work improves the level of dialogue, your effect on the organization will go beyond the help you offer your training participants.

You know great dialogue when you experience it. The level of engagement and energy far outshines the average business talk. Participants are actively thinking, listening, and contributing. Here are the elements of great training dialogue:

◆ **Relevance:** The topic of discussion is one that people care about and that makes a difference to their lives.

◆ **Inquiry:** Questions—both provocative and evocative—move the topic forward.

◆ **Freedom:** Participants feel free to share their ideas and thoughts, even those on the fringe. The conversation is open.

◆ **Connectedness:** There is a sense of shared purpose or interest. Participants feel connected to one another. All or most of the them are contributing.

◆ **Reception:** Participants listen well, interpret the information, provide feedback, and reinforce contribution.

◆ **Empowerment:** People feel they have some influence on the topic being discussed. Ideally, they can move the problem or opportunity forward, but they also can move the intellectual debate further.

◆ **Play:** The dialogue has a fluid energy to it and can be playful.

Great dialogue will have many or all of those characteristics. A work environment where people engage in lively dialogue will quickly solve problems and be better able to seize opportunities. As a trainer, you can help create an environment that encourages effective dialogue by addressing each one of those characteristics.

Ensuring Dialogue Relevance

When you work with managers, you'll want to focus on how the training material affects their daily challenges. If they're not engaged, then maybe the topic isn't relevant enough or you're not approaching it in a way that appeals to them. If you ask the right provocative or evocative questions, you should be able to grab their interest.

Creating Excellent Inquiry

Inquiry is at the core of training. Managers seek development because they want to explore and improve their effectiveness and learn more about their skills. Asking questions is a great way to jump-start inquiry. There are several types of questions, and they're not all treated equally. The two most common types of questions are closed-ended and open-ended.

- ◆ **Closed-ended questions:** Ask for a short or one-word answer. For example, "Do you want to be successful?"

- ◆ **Open-ended questions:** Ask for a longer, individualized answer. For example, "What would you like to accomplish this year?"

To create effective inquiry, you need to look deeper than whether the question is closed- or open-ended. Both types can be poor or excellent questions, although open-ended ones involve the client more. The two examples listed above are both poor questions. They're not interesting and they're much too general.

There's another way to look at creating inquiry that focuses on the quality of the questions you ask. As a trainer, you want to make sure that your questions are either provocative or evocative.

- **Provocative questions:** Excite and stimulate conversation. For example, "What would happen if . . . ?"

- **Evocative questions:** Pull participants in and help bring things to mind. For example, "What kind of work makes you feel most engaged and satisfied?"

Inquiry plays a significant role in learning. Select questions that move the topic forward and engage your training participants.

The Greek philosopher Socrates was well known for his provocative and evocative questioning style. Using the Socratic method of questioning can generate rich information that helps participants succeed, and using it in your training sessions can help managers develop critical thinking and creativity skills. Socratic questions enable trainers to create an intriguing and fruitful dialogue. The Socratic method emphasizes the use of thought-provoking questions to promote learning (instead of offering opinions and advice). A well-executed Socratic question stretches the mind and challenges widely held beliefs.

When it comes to training discussions, the more questions you ask, the better. But they need to be great questions. If you're comfortable sharing your opinions and ideas, your challenge will be to resist giving advice. Although advice may be helpful at times, it rarely improves inquiry. The most effective training will facilitate your trainees' thinking processes. To do this, try using Socratic questions.

Socratic questions are probing, and most are open-ended. You can use these questions in any situation. Inquiry creates change and is the cornerstone of training discussions because it helps participants think about and solve problems creatively. Socratic questions also will help them clarify what they understand and identify the issues about which they need more information. Throughout your training, these questions will bring to light new strategies and ideas. When you ask great questions, you create exciting dialogue that managers will find intrinsically motivating. Table 2.1 offers a sample list of Socratic questions.

Using Socratic questions to generate inquiry improves your ability to remain objective by facilitating managers' self-discoveries. The questions also expand the trainees' analyses of the situation and increase the number and quality of possibilities they

TABLE 2.1

Sample Questions Using the Socratic Method

Reason for Asking	Socratic Questions
To clarify your trainees' intents or motives	• Why do you want this outcome? • How will you benefit? • Why is this change important? • What gave you this idea? • Who will benefit from this change?
To ensure your trainees' goals are aligned for success	• How does this help you achieve your goal? • What does this mean to you? • What do you already know about this approach? • How does this change affect the other aspects of the organization?
To uncover your trainees' basic assumptions	• What other assumptions could also be valid? • Why do you believe this change is needed? • What does your peer/manager/team think about this situation? • What would happen if . . . ? • Why do you think I asked you this question?
To discover if your trainees have enough information	• What generalizations have you made? • How do you know that . . . ? • Why is this situation occurring? • Have you seen a situation similar to this before? • What verification is there to support your claim?
To help your trainees see other points of view	• What are the pros and cons of your approach? • How is this similar to or different from the way you have approached this in the past? • What would an opponent of the idea say? • What would your customers say? • How would your competitors approach this?

consider. Using Socratic questions increases the energy of the dialogue and improves your trainees' learning.

Encouraging the Freedom to Participate Fully

The effectiveness of your training dialogue can be crippled if you and your participants don't feel comfortable about being open and candid with each other. In a small-group training situation, you'll want to establish ground rules and manage participation so everyone is heard and all topics are considered. You may need to be the one to bring up a sensitive topic first to help break the ice for the rest of the group. Ensure that you deal diplomatically with over-participators or with comments that squash the group's creativity and engagement.

Ensuring Connectedness

Trainers sometimes walk the fine line between being involved but objective and being separated. Even so, you can be very connected to your training participants in that you take ownership of enabling their effectiveness through your training. Show an interest in their progress; show them that their successes matter to you. Being connected means having a strong and deep relationship. As a trainer, you want to be connected in a way that recognizes and honors each of your roles.

Improving Dialogue Reception

Many things get in the way of dialogue reception. Miscommunication, censored feedback, and poor listening can wreck a conversation. You may not hear what managers are trying to tell you, even if you hear the words they're speaking. Communication between two people goes through each person's filters. Figure 2.1 shows how messages change as they pass

FIGURE 2.1

How Filters Affect Communication

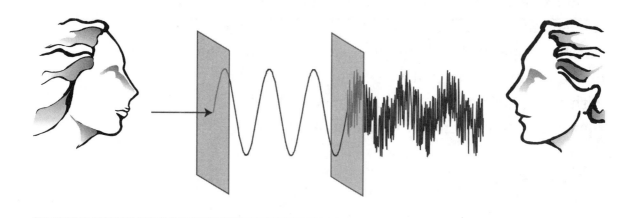

through the filters (mindset, biases, and opinions) of both the sender and the receiver.

If trainers don't listen to the words being said and hear the trainees' intentions, disconnects will occur. Even with the best of intentions, messages can become distorted and confused. Trainers who learn to listen well and provide effective feedback will improve overall dialogue reception.

Active and deep listening is a critical skill for trainers because so much of your work depends on clear communication and good relationships. It's a way of listening and responding to managers that improves mutual understanding. Many people are poor listeners. They get distracted, talk too much, and think about what they're going to say next when they should be concentrating on the speaker's words. Assuming they know what other people are going to say, they tune them out. It's challenging to take the time and energy to listen actively, but the rewards are worth the effort. You're listening actively when you

◆ demonstrate a sincere desire to pay attention to the other person (instead of mentally practicing what you're going to say next)

◆ commit to being coachable and open with the information being received from the other person

◆ relate to the other person's perspective, and empathize

◆ make an effort to understand the other person

◆ pay attention, and resist being distracted by other things in the environment

◆ ensure you have interpreted the message as intended through feedback, confirming, restating, or paraphrasing

◆ reflect on what the other person is saying

◆ synthesize the information, emotion, and feelings to improve understanding

◆ clarify the information by asking questions and probing

◆ validate perceptions and assumptions

- allow the other person to talk, uninterrupted

- focus on the other person, and be fully present.

Many people let full calendars, long to-do lists, stress, and their natural behavioral tendencies get in the way of active listening. To make a habit of listening actively, try these tips:

- Be with the other person, fully present and focused.

- Give the speaker good eye contact; don't let your eyes roam around the room.

- Take some notes, but don't look at other papers or reports. Don't take such detailed notes that you're missing the overall message.

- Let the other person talk, and don't worry about filling the lulls between sentences.

- Ask clarifying questions.

- Mentally put yourself in the other person's shoes.

- Respond to what the other person is saying.

- Eliminate distractions like phone, pager, and email pings.

Active listening is a habit that you can *and must* develop. Being a great listener benefits you as a trainer by reducing misunderstandings, improving information accuracy, and ensuring that you have complete information from which to work. Managers open up more to people who listen well.

Improving Topic Empowerment

When training conversations focus on the topics that are most important to managers, achieving topic empowerment generally isn't a problem. If training participants don't feel they can make changes or use the suggested techniques, they may feel disconnected from the discussion. It's important that you help participants connect with the content and determine how it applies to their work; otherwise, they may tune out or become frustrated. Topic empowerment is important because we want managers to feel they can make a difference—because they can!

Keeping Conversations Playful

You can do a lot of things that will keep your training discussions playful. A playful conversation doesn't need to lack seriousness. In this context, playfulness means playing with ideas, concepts, and information in a way that keeps the conversation's energy level high. Here are several ways you can improve conversation playfulness:

◆ Ask participants to read interesting and provocative articles prior to the training.

◆ Change the climate of the training session to one that's intellectually stimulating.

- Mindmap (that is, use pictures, lines, boxes, and arrows to diagram) the conversation.

- Share a success story of someone with a similar goal.

- Use idea-generation techniques.

- Plan the training agenda so the meeting moves quickly and flows well. Put an attention grabber at the beginning, and try to plan for a high point to occur toward the end of the meeting.

- Make homework assignments that are unconventional and intriguing. For example, ask participants to contact their role models. Suggest that they change one behavior for one week. Suggest a thought-provoking movie or live performance that relates to the topic being discussed.

To make conversations more playful, have a variety of contexts and types of information coming together. Tap into the interests and needs of your participants and offer information that will stretch and broaden their perspectives.

Training is more art than science. It's a dialogue that you drive and keep focused on the learners. Effective training produces energy. Whether participants leave your training sessions with more energy and excitement depends on the quality of the dialogue. Great dialogue is stimulating, intriguing, and enlightening; and the best trainers make this happen in a seamless, almost magical way.

As I wrote at the beginning of this chapter, I could list a bunch of skills that will help you be a great management trainer. There are many qualities that are useful—organization, sense of urgency, ease in speaking before groups, and consultation skills are just a few. That said, I honestly believe that if you've been a successful manager, have business acumen, passionately want to be a learning catalyst, and can facilitate great conversations, you have the necessary ingredients to be a great management trainer. Focus on developing these areas, and you'll have achieved the 20 percent that will produce 80 percent of your management training results.

CHAPTER THREE

Making the Most of *10 Steps to Be a Successful Manager*

I've created this review based on the assumption that you know how to train people. I won't bore you with fundamental training techniques in this *Facilitator's Guide*. What I think would be more helpful to you is to share my underlying assumptions and intentions for the material presented in *10 Steps to Be a Successful Manager* so you can modify and apply it to suit your needs. That's the kind of background information I most appreciate when I'm planning and preparing for training sessions.

With that aim in mind, I've reviewed each of the 10 steps individually and, for each step, I'll share the following in this chapter:

◆ **Author's notes:** my overall goal for this step and the beliefs that fueled its writing; some commentary on the overall theme and key messages

- ◆ **Discussion topics:** ways to generate lively and helpful conversations about the step material

- ◆ **Activity suggestions:** ideas for getting participants to explore and try step techniques.

Before I begin the step-by-step review, I want to share the overall underlying beliefs and assumptions at the heart of *10 Steps to Be a Successful Manager* and of this *Facilitator's Guide*. I believe that we can respond in ways that move us closer to our goals, or we can choose actions that move us in the opposite direction. I've created a group of responses that I think improve results. I call them *results-oriented responses* (RORs). Take a look at table 3.1: The ROR Cheat Sheet. It compares results-oriented responses with low-results responses. The RORs I cover there are the basic philosophies at the center of *10 Steps to Be a Successful Manager.*

Of all the tools I've created, the ROR Cheat Sheet is one of my favorites. Use it whenever you feel stuck or like you're not making the progress you want. It's also a great tool to use when coaching!

OK, now on to the nitty-gritty. The suggestions and techniques offered below reinforce and encourage the RORs.

TABLE 3.1

ROR Cheat Sheet

Results-Oriented Response	Low-Results Response
Being an owner: Assumes responsibility for the outcome. Takes initiative to make things better. Does whatever it takes to get ideal results. Commits one's heart and engages one's mind.	**Being a custodian:** Does only what is required. Waits for others to act. Hopes someone else will take ownership. Avoids whatever is unpleasant. Behaves compliantly. Does not fully engage heart and mind.
Being active: Takes the initiative to get things done. Is not easily deterred by setbacks. Is proactive. When barriers are present, immediately identifies them and implements an alternative action plan.	**Being passive:** Won't take action unless told to do so. Acts only when necessary. Is reactive in stance and style. Doesn't act when faced with barriers and setbacks.
Taking generative action: Generates new and better alternative approaches and carries them out. Creates from unlimited possibilities. Does not get stuck on how things are already being done.	**Being automatic:** Sticks with the way things have always been done; preserves the status quo. Prefers to act by habit, and won't move out of his or her comfort zone. Does not create new approaches or solutions.
Keeping promises: Does what is promised. Fulfills commitments. Keeps his or her word.	**Breaking promises or commitments:** Does not follow through with what she or he has promised or committed to. Lets to-do items build up beyond the date expected. Does not follow through on real or implied agreements.
Influencing through enrollment: Influences others by helping them see, understand, and take ownership of the goal for themselves. Demonstrates the strategy and plan in such a way that others see and take on the vision for themselves. Prompts others to be committed and passionate about the vision and plan.	**Influencing through subtle coercion:** Communicates the vision and plan in a way that resembles a directive or a suggestion. Influences others by making them feel they need to accept and conform. This type of influencing others rarely results in committed and passionate performance.
Being service oriented: Sees her or his role as one that provides service to others. Facilitates cooperation, commitment, and learning. Manages from the mindset that asks, What can I do to help others excel today?	**Expecting to be served:** Sees his or her role as one in which people should serve him or her. This stance limits the capacity to have an impact on others. Manages from the mindset that asks, What have you done for me today?
Being coachable: Accepts and uses feedback, input, criticism, and ideas from others; and is curiously observant. Is not defensive when given feedback. Recognizes that others have something to offer.	**Being uncoachable:** Blocks the environment from being influential; puts up barriers. Focuses more on being right, looking good, and appearing in charge.
Practicing quality dialogue: Communicates with the intent of making a difference or moving a topic forward. Engages in active conversation focused on the topic at hand.	**Using dialogue without purpose:** Communicates in a way that does not move the topic forward. Spends time discussing rumors, gossip, complaints, diversions; whines; offers opinions that aren't helpful for enabling the desired result.

Trainer's Notes

Author's Notes

Step 1: Clarify, Negotiate, and Commit to Your Role

I've met a lot of managers who just don't get it. They don't understand their role and don't know why they are in the role. They think they know, but their thoughts are way off the mark. To be fair, not all managers are like this, but I would say that most are not quite fully aware of the reasons why they're in that position and the purpose for their role. That's a shame because most managers are smart, hard-working people and I hate to see their efforts wasted.

I'm guessing that a lot of people will read Step 1 and think it's too basic. I hope you can help people stay in the step a while and dig deep into the conversation about expectations. My goal in writing this step is to get more people talking about fundamental expectations. When you coach executives, you hear their hopes and dreams for what their talented managers will do for the company. Here's the problem—I don't think these managers have ever heard these hopes and dreams. In fact, I think if they did know what the boss really wanted, they would make different choices about how they spend their time.

My personal pet peeve is when managers don't understand that they have an obligation to model that which they seek in the organization. I've worked with far too many managers who just didn't get it that they ought to be the role model of excellence. The few who do get it are the rock stars for whom everyone wants to work. They're amazing people who make significant contributions to their companies. I believe this to be true for HR and training professionals, too. We need to show people how excellence looks, acts, and sounds. How can we expect to influence and inspire others unless we are amazing role models?

I also think it's interesting for managers to get a feel for how expectations are different among their manager, peers, and team members. You'll notice throughout the book that I suggest managers include peers in conversations. A group of peer managers can be a powerful team driving the culture and results forward. The more managers work together and in alignment, the better their teams will cooperate.

The topic of negotiating expectations might be met with a few jeers. Some managers may feel they can't negotiate—but, really, they need to do it. If they're being asked to make the impossible happen, it's important that a conversation occurs about that.

Step 1 is aimed at getting managers in a mindset that acknowledges the importance of the managerial role and their potential to make a significant contribution to the organization. I would love to see this topic catalyze more open and candid conversations about managerial expectations. The work invested here will pay off when it comes time for the managers to communicate expectations to their team members.

Discussion Topics for Step 1

◆ How can you be sure we understand what's expected of us? How do you do this?

◆ Do you know the one thing your boss/closest peer/team member wishes you would do differently?

◆ How do fundamental expectations change what you do on a daily basis? Should they?

◆ Do any of you feel that the expectations others have of you are conflicting or unrealistic?

◆ What do you think of the list of expectations for all managers?

◆ What do you think the author was getting at with the section on committing to our roles? Is this really a challenge? Have you seen managers who have struggled to commit to their roles? What does that look like?

Activity Suggestions for Step 1

◆ If possible, structure your training so that everyone has two or three of the expectations conversations prior to coming to training. Process the activity in the training session, asking people about what they learned, how the conversations felt, and if there were any surprises. Try to get a feel for how open and candid the conversations were.

◆ If you have a group of peers in the training session, select several questions and have them conduct peer interviews regarding expectations. Give each person three meaty questions (different questions for each peer in the pair), and allow 30 minutes for both sides of the conversation. Process the activity.

◆ Ask each manager to identify three to five key expectations, and then to create her or his own Management Filter. Pass out the blank management filter worksheets (worksheet 1.1 from the book), and give participants 20 minutes to complete the form. Ask them to share their forms in a small group of three or four people for a total of 15 minutes. Assign managers the homework of using the filter for two weeks. If training extends over multiple sessions, check back with participants on whether the filter was helpful, and in what ways.

Trainer's Notes

Author's Notes

Step 2: Understand Your Expected Results

This is one of my favorite steps! If more managers defined their goals and tasks in terms of grand-slam home runs, we'd see amazing things happen. I know that you understand the magic behind this philosophy, but I'll summarize here just to reinforce it:

> **Self-fulfilling prophecy or Pygmalion effect:** Once you establish an expectation, even if it isn't accurate, you act in ways that are consistent with that expectation. Your expectations often determine what becomes reality.

The self-fulfilling prophecy can be helpful or unhelpful. When managers assume that they'll fail, they're often right. The managers' failures occur not because those were the likely outcomes, but because the managers' brains were tuned for defeat. To combat the negative self-fulfilling prophecy, managers need to pay attention to and reprogram destructive self-talk. By acknowledging the power of the self-fulfilling prophecy, managers can create and employ a more positive model. Setting grand-slam home run goals puts an entirely different energy and vibe into the work.

When managers define goals, projects, and tasks in terms of what a grand-slam home run would look like, they'll achieve more than if they didn't define excellence. Try this yourself for your training goals. Better yet, set specific grand-slam home run goals for *this* training. I'd love it if you did that! And you would get better results from the training because your thoughts and actions would be tuned to excellence.

When I work with managers, I often need to help them reframe their definition of results and results orientation. The step starts off with a discussion of the traditional definitions of the term **results.** We talk about business results so much that we've made the term useless. Anyone can produce an outcome—which is a result. To me, that's mediocre. Let's help people move beyond being satisfied with a result; let's inspire managers to create grand slams. I love the HR example, don't you? I've been an HR director, so please don't take the example as a cut against HR. I think the HR department can make a huge positive difference—but not if it's focused on days to hire as a measure of success.

The purpose of this step is to help managers see greater possibilities and to embrace taking on extraordinary contribution.

Discussion Topics for Step 2

◆ What might be the downsides of defining goals in terms of grand-slam home runs? What are the benefits?

◆ Have you experienced a grand slam? How did it look and feel?

◆ How many of you would like to define grand-slam goals for your peers?

Activity Suggestions for Step 2

◆ Ask people to define their goals in terms of grand-slam home runs, and then share the goals with their peers in the training session. Encourage them to expand their thinking and not just add to the goal. A grand slam is amazing. What would make the implementation of each task or goal extraordinary?

◆ For added ummph, prepare a set of scorecards (1 through 10) for each participant. Distribute the card sets and ask one participant at a time to stand up and share one grand-slam goal. Instruct the rest of the participants to rate the "grand-slamness" of each goal by holding up a scorecard (10 being the highest rating).

Trainer's Notes

Author's Notes

Step 3: Know Your Piece of the Business

Creating good metrics challenges a lot of managers. As a matter of fact, I've seen training departments struggle with this, too. We often create measures because we need something to write on the yearly goals forms or performance evaluations. Sometimes we select measures because they're the easiest ones to track. Here's the problem—most of the measures we put on performance evaluations don't tell us how well our functions are running.

In Step 3, I'd like managers to think about how they know when things are going well or not well, and how they know why things are going well or not well. The question "Are we making a difference" is important.

I love the Geoffrey Canada example in the book because it provides a compelling example of courage. Sometimes we need to admit that we're not making a difference. When we can do this, we open things up for a breakthrough. Think about this in terms of your management development programs. How do you know they're working? Are you making a difference? I shared my thoughts on measuring management development in Step 1 of this *Facilitator's*

Guide. The difference I want to make with this step is to help managers define their success indicators and then use those indicators to make daily choices about time and priorities.

Discussion Topics for Step 3

◆ How many of you believe you have adequate measures that tell you how well your department is performing? Ask for examples.

◆ How do you know when you're measuring the right things? What are some of the clues that the measurement might not be the right one on which to focus?

◆ Ask participants to read the example (or summarize it for them) that opens this step in the book. How can you make sure that you and your team aren't caught going full speed in the wrong direction like that company?

Activity Suggestions for Step 3

◆ Ask participants to hold the team meeting described in the book (using worksheet 3.1) prior to the training session. In the training session, discuss the outcomes of that meeting.

◆ Ask participants to write down the two most important metrics that tell them how well their function is performing. Then ask them to share these two metrics in a small group of peers. Instruct the peers to ask questions or challenge the metrics if they don't seem like the right ones. Encourage people to disagree in order to help each other discover the right metrics. Allow 10 minutes of discussion for each person's metrics, or more if needed. Ask people to share what they learned.

Trainer's Notes

Author's Notes
Step 4: Build a Great Team

In Step 4 I hope to broaden and deepen managers' views on the dynamics that make for a great team. In particular, I've chosen to focus on the value of diversity, healthy challenge (productive irreverence), and collaboration. All of those positive traits can only happen when managers develop an environment of openness and candor, and that's why I start the step off with a discussion of building relationships. Attending weekly team meetings doesn't constitute working together, and generally it doesn't lead to team members really getting to know one another either. That's why I encourage managers to assign subteams and pairs to work on tasks together. When we work together, we build relationships.

I've heard managers lament that their teams suffer from low morale or energy, but I don't always see that they're making a connection between the low energy and their management of the group. To enliven minds, we need to manage in a way that creates a stimulating environment. Although it is clearly harder, I do believe you can have a positive and energetic team in an organization that's suffering overall. Managers make the difference, but do our managers see that?

My favorite part of this step is the bit on productive irreverence. Can you tell? I hope that this section will encourage managers to be more productively irreverent and to see the productive irreverence of others as a helpful gift (not as a nuisance). Perhaps you can encourage a little productive irreverence in the training session!

I'd also like managers to think about the productivity aspect of collaboration. Few teams collaborate, but more should. Collaboration can happen in pairs and in smaller teams (this will reinforce relationship building, too). Merely getting a few ideas from people does *not* constitute collaboration. Collaborating means co-owning a process and an outcome.

Discussion Topics for Step 4

- ◆ Looking at the second paragraph in Step 4, how many of you would say your teams fit that description? In what ways? If not, why not?

- ◆ Are you productively irreverent? Tell me the last time you demonstrated productive irreverence, and describe what happened. Does our company culture nurture or squelch productive irreverence? How can we create a culture that nurtures it?

- ◆ How often do you collaborate with your peers—really collaborate? Do your team members regularly collaborate?

- ◆ In this step I shared an example of a manager who found a five-to-one improvement in team productivity when members collaborated. What kind of productivity improvements do you think you would see if your teams collaborated more?

◆ Does your organization structure and physical layout encourage collaboration? What can you do to help collaboration happen in natural and informal ways?

◆ Do you coddle people who don't get along with each other? In what ways? Why? What should you do about your tendency to coddle others?

Activity Suggestions for Step 4

◆ Have participants identify one task or project that would benefit from peer collaboration. Ask each person to stand up and describe the project or task, and then ask for a peer in the room to volunteer to collaborate on this task. Each person should volunteer only once. It's OK if the pairings end up seeming a bit odd—like a marketing manager collaborating with a manufacturing manager. In fact, the odd pairings might make for better results. Ask participants to schedule the first collaboration meeting within a week and to follow through with collaborating on this task.

◆ Ask small groups to create a Management Filter (like the one used in Step 1) for creating strong teams. Copy the blank filter on an overhead transparency (if you still own one of these ancient beasts) so that each team can share its filters. As a follow-up, type the teams' filters and email them to participants. Discuss the similarities that show up across various teams' filters.

Trainer's Notes

Author's Notes

Step 5: Choose Employees Wisely

I firmly believe that our ability to choose the right people is a huge asset in ensuring team excellence. Notice I used the word, *right* in that last sentence and a lot in the step. The key to selection is finding the person who is the best fit—that's "right" in my mind. I know that some HR folks might not agree will some of the ideas I suggest in this step, but that's OK—I'm being productively irreverent. The key messages I'd like managers to hear are that they need to own employee selection and they ought not settle for someone who's not the right fit.

Defining the right fit isn't always straightforward. Sometimes the culture of the company presents challenges that make fit a complex issue. Your organizational idiosyncrasies need to be considered when defining the criteria for fit. Encourage participants to peel back the layers of what it really takes to be successful in your organization.

Interviewing—what fun! Well, often it isn't fun and I hope that my comments and suggestions are a bit provocative. It may be a lot of work to develop relationships with interviewees, but, in my book, anything less isn't enough. The hiring process should always feel personal, even when that's a pain in the neck. The better and more voluminous the conversations, the better your chances of determining fit.

Do you like the behavioral interviewing and reference check questions I offered? Some of them are basic, and some a bit more ambitious. I hope managers will see that their questions ought to go deeper than asking about specific experiences or previous jobs.

The last part of the step is short, but important. When a manager accepts a candidate for a position, a new relationship is starting—one that everyone hopes will last years. That's exciting! Make sure that new people come in with a bang.

Discussion Topics for Step 5

- Looking at the sample behavioral questions for management candidates (example 5.1), which questions would you have a tough time answering? Why? Are there any questions you might like to ask your next interviewees?

- What are some organizational or cultural idiosyncrasies that you need to think about when determining fit? How should those characteristics affect who you select for open positions?

- How many interviews is enough?

- Think about a hiring decision you've made (or that a peer or manager has made) that you would do differently if you could go back in time. What did you miss? What questions would you ask now that you didn't ask then? What would you do differently that would have yielded a different result?

Activity Suggestion for Step 5

◆ I love this exercise. As a part of the pre-work for the training session, ask any managers who currently have open positions to bring five copies of the job description for the open position. Put the participants into groups of four. Each group will be assigned one real job opening for this exercise (if you have too many managers with open positions, ask for volunteers for the right number of positions). Ask each group to create (1) criteria for job fit, (2) a meaty list of interview questions designed to determine candidate fit, (3) and an interview design process that will produce the best results. Give each team 60 minutes to do this work (more if needed); then have each team share its work with the class. Invite someone from HR to roam the groups as a support person and to provide ideas and suggestions as needed. The output is real and helpful!

Trainer's Notes

Author's Notes

Step 6: Define and Model Excellence

I love this step, too. Defining excellence is so powerful. Just as we want to know what a grand slam looks like, our team members want to know—and deserve to know—how they can achieve what we consider to be excellence. I'm all for inclusion and empowerment, but it's important that managers share *their* definitions of excellence with their teams. We all need to know how our manager sees things—right or wrong and whether we agree or not. In fact, it's more important to know when we disagree. I think you could spend a day on just this step.

The section about acting consistently with our definitions of excellence is very important. I'm sure you've seen this, too: Managers say one thing with their mouths and then say the opposite with their actions and decisions. I've challenged entire leadership teams on this concept. They said, "We won't tolerate unproductive behavior," but then they not only tolerated it, they reinforced it with their actions (and inaction).

When I consult with a company, I like to talk to a bunch of people, observe the working environment, and then tell them their definition of excellence. What a shocker! The differences between how they think they define excellence and how they actually define excellence in action are often significant.

And that doesn't happen because these managers are stupid or evil people. We all do this on some level. The only way to bring actions and intentions closer together is to be conscious about what we're doing and make better choices. That's the kind of introspection and action that I hope this step will provoke.

I like the example of a definition of excellence that I created for a client. Have you noticed that a lot of my examples are focused on management? It's my devious way of reinforcing those RORs again. The example offers a good starting point for any group, and is a good object for classroom conversation.

Discussion Topics for Step 6

◆ Do your employees know what excellent performance looks like?

◆ When it comes to defining excellence, what's one hope or goal that would be very high on your list?

◆ How do you help your team members understand how you evaluate excellence?

◆ Think about all the things you did yesterday. Did you do or say anything that could be interpreted as conflicting with your definition of excellence?

Activity Suggestions for Step 6

◆ Have participants write definitions of excellence for their teams, using worksheet 6.1 from the book. Give them 20 minutes to work; then pair them up and encourage them to share what they've written, offer ideas, and cheat off each other's lists. Ask for a couple volunteers to read their definitions to the whole group.

◆ Ask participants to review table 6.1 from the book, and then take 10 minutes to create their own list of potential conflicting behaviors to watch out for. This is a list of three to five actions that would do the greatest damage in contradicting their definitions of excellence. It's their "must-not-do" cheat sheet. Ask a few people to read their lists.

◆ Ask participants to create a plan for using the work they've done during this session to ensure their teams are clear about excellence. This is a brief action plan—allow 10 minutes.

Trainer's Notes

Author's Notes

Step 7: Plan the Work and Work the Plan—Flexibly

Many managers are lousy planners! It's because they're so darned busy and their to-do lists become all consuming. Another reason managers don't plan well is that the existing standards for managers are too low.

In this step I just touch the surface of planning. I could have gone much deeper but decided to stick with two easy ways to start planning better—the weekly and daily planning regimens. Before you do this training, give these two planning habits a try yourself. They really do work.

The objectives of this step are easy and straightforward: Get managers to do the weekly and daily planning, and get them to share their plans with team members. If they just do that, their work will be much more focused and fruitful.

Discussion Topics for Step 7

◆ Describe your current planning regimens—how do you plan your work?

◆ How many of you would say you spend enough time on planning? For those who don't, what gets in the way? What are the consequences? For those of you who do spend enough time, describe what you do.

◆ How do you share work plans with your team? How do you keep your team informed of priorities and changes?

◆ How many of you know there's a project or task on your to-do list right now that ought to be killed? What's the best way to get rid of such tasks?

◆ As a team of peers, how can you help each other keep project and task lists free of obsolete or low-value-added work?

Activity Suggestions for Step 7

◆ Have each participant do a weekly plan and then a daily plan. These should be real-world plans for the upcoming week and the next day. Allow 25 minutes or more to complete both. Encourage participants to ask peers questions or solicit ideas or feedback.

◆ Group the participants into teams of peers who work together in some way. Have them do a 15-minute standing huddle in which they quickly share their weekly and daily plans with each other and then ask whatever clarifying questions are needed. Process the exercise by asking what they learned and how the huddle format worked. Suggest they continue the peer huddles (and team huddles) back on the job.

Trainer's Notes

Author's Notes

Step 8: Obliterate Barriers

Obliterating barriers is a great way to spend an afternoon. When I was a manager, getting rid of mucky muck was one of my favorite things to do each day. With this step I hope to inspire managers to embrace their barrier-busting role. Removing hassles from the workplace is a very satisfying thing to do!

I also think it's helpful to build a culture of barrier obliteration. How tolerant of dysfunction is your organization? You know it sucks the life out of people, right? Does your company wear people out? If so, taking on the task of creating a barrier-free culture could make a huge difference in how people feel at work. And when they feel good, they work good (I know that's bad grammar, but I like the sound of it).

What are the barriers to this training? Perhaps you can start the positive process by removing them. Then tell your story as an example.

Discussion Topics for Step 8

◆ In your organization, would you say that people generally experience a lot of barriers, or only a few? Why? Are there areas that deal with more mucky muck?

◆ What kind of mucky muck most gets in your way each day?

◆ How do you determine what's hindering your team members' performance? What methods or techniques work best for you to identify and eliminate barriers?

Activity Suggestions for Step 8

◆ Here's a really productive activity. Ask each participant to describe the two greatest barriers to their ability to do their best work. In groups of four or five, ask participants to share their descriptions and then offer each other suggestions for getting rid of each barrier. Allow five minutes of conversation per barrier, two barriers per person, for a total of about 50 minutes. One ground rule: The team can't move on to the next barrier until it comes up with at least two viable ideas. In other words, they can't just say, "Geez, that's a tough one, I don't know," and move on.

◆ Ask participants to do what I suggest in the Tune Up and Realign section at the end of Step 8 as pre-work for the class session. Ask small groups to share their lists and come up with the five most common barriers to productivity, and then identify five strategies to obliterate each of the five barriers. Allow 30 minutes of working time and then ask each team to share. Notice the differences and similarities. Have a conversation about what this management group ought to do about the most common forms of mucky muck. Have them leave the training room with a real plan. If it involves sharing their findings with the next level of management, have them book that meeting before they leave the training session. Better yet, invite a member of senior management into the class to hear their thoughts and ideas.

Trainer's Notes

Author's Notes

Step 9: Proactively Manage Change and Transition

As I mentioned at the beginning of this step, I'm a strong proponent of Bridges Transition Model. If change is a big issue for your organization, buy copies of *Managing Transitions* for all your managers. There's an exercise at the beginning of that book that would make for a great training session discussion.

I really want managers to embrace transition management. I've seen a lot of problems caused by people and teams who failed to transition—they're stuck in the endings and not moving forward.

The major mistakes managers make are failing to communicate enough, and not including people as much as possible in planning for and implementing change. I think we also coddle some people too much. If someone chooses not to change, even with help, support, and communication, then he or she may no longer be a good fit for the organization. But all too often we let that person languish and the team is dragged down as a result. We can't know whether someone simply won't change or just needs a little help unless we manage transitions more effectively.

Discussion Topics for Step 9

- How many of you would say that you or one of your team members is stuck in transition (stuck in endings or in the neutral zone)?

- What does being stuck in the endings phase look like here?

- What techniques have you used to help people adjust to changes?

- When you and your manager plan changes, how much time do you spend planning for helping people transition? What should you be doing together as a peer management team that could help people transition?

Activity Suggestions for Step 9

- This step is best discussed before a major change implementation. Involve the team of managers and ask them to create a plan for managing and facilitating changes. The plan should include action to take before, during, and after the change is implemented. Make sure that they include communicating the 4Ps.

- Get participants to practice communicating the 4Ps. Have them select an upcoming change and create a five- to 10-minute presentation that goes over the 4Ps. Have them

practice the presentation with each other
and offer feedback and ideas for increasing
clarity and team member participation. Allow 20 minutes to create the presentation
and five to 10 minutes each for the sharing.

Trainer's Notes

Author's Notes

Step 10: Leave a Legacy of Cpacity to Produce

This is a fun step because it focuses on the positive mark we want to leave—our legacy. It's crucial that we think about our legacy now because our vision of the future will guide our current choices and actions. If we're guided by a powerful vision, our results and impact will reflect it. If we fail to create a vision of our legacy, daily transactions and to-do lists will guide us. That's not so powerful.

I also like asking managers to think about their legacy because many have never thought about it before. You can see the wheels spinning in their heads, and their whole demeanor changes when they define their legacy.

One clarification: I'm not suggesting that the vision we create today will be the legacy we leave. Things change and so will our vision and impact. Even so, if we have a powerful and inspiring vision, it will take us to wonderful places.

I wrote the piece about leaving things better than the way we got them to encourage everyone to think about taking the high road when they leave the company. Chances are, if you have a training session of 25 managers, at least a few are currently thinking about leaving, so the point is well timed.

Discussion Topics for Step 10

◆ How many of you have thought about the legacy you want to leave as manager? What would some of you like to accomplish?

◆ How many of you know the legacy your manager would like to leave? Would you like to know that?

◆ What's one way that your manager's current actions and words reinforce her or his vision for the legacy she or he will leave?

Activity Suggestions for Step 10

◆ Have participants create their vision for the legacy they want to leave as manager. Encourage them to work together or ask for input and to help each other polish and practice their visions. Ask each participant to stand up and share with the class the legacy he or she wishes to leave. Encourage them to share their visions with their manager and team members as well.

◆ Ask participants to define three ways that they can begin to "be" their legacy today—ways of being that would be in alignment with their legacy vision.

CHAPTER FOUR

Informal Training Ideas

10 Steps to Be a Successful Manager lends itself well for use with a variety of training and development formats. In this chapter, I'll share several informal training ideas. Truth be told, these ideas are my favorites. As I mentioned in chapter 1, I believe that creating stimulating conversations and getting people to try techniques using real-world situations are the most powerful ways to improve application and habituation.

After training for 25 years, and being certified in more programs than I can count using both hands, I've come to believe that informal training is best. The conversations tend to be more authentic, the agenda less mechanistic and controlled, and the atmosphere more personal and fun. (Because I know that informal training isn't always practical, in the next chapter I've included several sample agendas for daylong or multiday training sessions.)

Management Coaching

Do you provide coaching to managers? Many of the managers I've coached have lacked fundamental management skills and habits—the stuff in *10 Steps to Be a Successful Manager*. I'm not a big fan of regimented coaching processes; I prefer to keep things organic, flexible, and real. That said, if I were to coach a manager who needs to develop fundamental management skills, I'd use *10 Steps to Be a Successful Manager* in a heartbeat.

If the manager needs to develop or redevelop fundamental skills, start from the top and go over Steps 1 and 2, and then cover any other steps that apply. Assign pre-work and homework for each coaching session so you have something meaty to discuss. Use the step-specific discussion questions and activities from chapter 3 of this *Facilitator's Guide*, as appropriate, to meet the manager's needs. Table 4.1 shows how I'd assign the pre-work and homework to cover the first two steps.

I'm a big proponent of assigning pre-work and homework for coaching sessions and all forms of informal training. The conversations are much better when participants are prepared. Also, learning begins with the reading. Some people will have tried out the techniques by the time the coaching session or training meeting is held—a win–win for sure! When working one-on-one or in small groups (which

TABLE 4.1

Coaching Pre-work, Session Work, and Homework Assignments for Steps 1 and 2

Coaching Session	Pre-work	Activities during the Session	Homework
First	Read the Introduction and Steps 1 and 2 of *10 Steps to Be a Successful Manager*	Discuss the material in the Introduction and the two steps. Prepare the manager for holding the expectations meetings and home-run goals meeting. Go over the Management Filter (example 1.1) and grand-slam matrix (example 2.1).	Schedule and have expectations meetings with manager and team members (also with peers, if time permits). When meeting with the manager about expectations, also define key grand-slam home run deliverables. Fill out the Management Filter and grand-slam goals matrix before the next coaching session.
Second	None	Review the homework. Spend at least an hour discussing the filter and matrix. Notice how they fit together. Discuss whether the manager feels the expectations and goals are realistic. Help him or her plan to negotiate expectations if needed.	Share your understanding of the expectations with your manager and team members. Share your key deliverables and grand-slam goals with your manager and team members. Notice their reactions. Review your Management Filter each morning.
Third	None	Go over the homework. If the manager hasn't done that work, reassign it. Offer to facilitate the meetings, if needed.	None

I prefer), I find that people do their homework. They know that they'll be expected to participate.

Several sections of the *10 Steps* book will work well with your management coaching practice. Steps 6 (Define and Model Excellence) and 7 (Plan the Work and Work the Plan—Flexibly) fit together nicely, and can be covered over two to three coaching sessions. Step 10 (Leave a Legacy of Capacity to Produce) should dovetail into your conversations about goal setting and vision.

Use *10 Steps* as a tool to help augment your management coaching practice. I think you'll find that the book's main messages support the development goals you and your manager clients will establish.

Book Club and Brown-Bag Book Discussions

The informal discussion group is perhaps my favorite training format for management development topics. In groups of five to 12 people, it's easy to have great conversations, build relationships, and test and apply techniques. In addition, people in small, informal groups tend to be more internally motivated to attend (versus large, formal training programs that rely on extrinsic motivation to ensure attendance). The source of motivation makes all the difference in the world to me. At this point in my career, I refuse to do training that's forced because I know it's a waste of time. Sure, there are some compliance requirements for certain types of training, but that's not the kind of training I do. In the arena of management training, forcing people to attend training is generally a colossal waste of energy and resources. Avoid doing that if you can.

The most common type of book club or brown-bag session I've held meets once a week for 90-120 minutes. Often, the meeting is held midday and people bring their lunches to the discussion (that's the brown-bag part). As the facilitator, I bring a sweet treat for the end—something like fruit, cookies, brownies, or caramel apples. Let me just say that this type of training produces a huge return-on-investment for the following reasons:

◆ The results generally are better than in traditional training classroom settings.

◆ There's a great opportunity to build peer relationships—better cooperation and collaboration will occur.

◆ The costs are low! You can use a small conference room, and your only costs are copies of the book you're using as a text (*10 Steps*, for example) and dessert.

◆ Your prep time is minimal. You can begin new series at any time or hold more than one at a time.

◆ You can include telecommuting managers via a conference call.

One department manager I worked with decided to hold informal trainings during the time he generally set aside for staff meetings. The staff was already in a habit of meeting each week at that time, so substituting informal training disrupted no one's schedule. What a huge success!

A word of caution: Please don't create Microsoft PowerPoint presentations for informal training sessions. Projected presentations take the "informal" right out of a session. Informal means *informal.* Have some handouts, copies of articles, and rough talking points, but the conversations should be pretty relaxed. Let the group take the content in the direction that's most interesting and helpful. Go where the energy is.

That said, informal does not have to mean lax. I assign pre-reading and homework every week. I want participants doing most of the activities I outlined in chapter 3 of this *Facilitator's Guide.*

Some of the 10 steps can be covered in a single 90-minute session; some may take two sessions (most of the work occurs during the pre-work and homework). How much time each step requires depends, in part, on your group, its needs, and its interests. That said, here's an initial breakdown that you can use as a starting point:

◆ Introduction and Steps 1 and 2—put these together as pre-reading; then do the activities and discuss the material over three informal sessions.

◆ Step 3—one session.

◆ Step 4—one session.

◆ Step 5—one session.

◆ Steps 6 and 7 —put these together as pre-reading; then do the activities and discuss the material over three informal sessions.

- Step 8—one session.

- Step 9—one session, unless there's a major change coming soon; if there is a change in the offing, take more time with this step.

- Step 10—one session.

It's important that you not try to defend the book if people disagree with parts of it or with specific techniques. The more lively and open the discussion, the better. Encourage alternative ideas and suggestions, and reinforce people who express doubts or concerns. Invite them to reinvent a technique if it doesn't work for them. You want this kind of productive irreverence because your training will be more effective as a result of being challenged and reformed.

There are many variations to the informal training group. Here are several structures that have worked for me:

- weekly 90-minute sessions

- biweekly two-hour sessions

- monthly two-hour sessions

- weekly 30-minute sessions, with the daily reinforcement of an internal blog

- weekly teleseminars for geographically dispersed groups.

Use the structure that works best for your managers. You want them to attend on a consistent basis because they want to be there; and you want them to participate and do the work. Adjust the time, place, and logistics to best meet those goals.

CHAPTER FIVE

Sample Training Agendas

10 Steps to Be a Successful Manager makes an excellent text for management development sessions. I wrote the book with its use as a training aid in mind. Each step offers a concept, techniques, and suggestions for applying those techniques. That's also a logical training sequence—present the concept, discuss techniques, practice the techniques. Refer to the discussion questions and suggested activities offered in chapter 3 of this *Facilitator's Guide* for more ideas.

As I mentioned earlier, my assumption is that you know how to train, so I'm not getting overly prescriptive with the agendas. I assume you'll take the ideas and create your training agendas based on what works best for your managers.

As you read in the previous chapter, I'm a big fan of informal training, but I know that's not always practical. That's why I've put together several sample training agendas for you to consider. I encourage you to make your training sessions look and feel more informal and organic, even if you're putting thousands of managers through the same programs. I shared several suggestions for improving application in chapter 1 of this facilitator's guide, so reread that chapter before your trainings, if you think it will help.

Timelines

◆ **One day**—with lunch and breaks, I count a full day as six hours of training.

◆ **Two-day**—with lunches and breaks, for a total of 12 hours of training.

◆ **One week**—with lunches, breaks, and finishing a bit earlier on the last day, I count a week as 28 hours of training.

Sample Agenda for a One-Day Training

Please don't try to cover the whole book in one day. It would not be possible to create a learning environment conducive to repeated application if you tried to address all 10 steps in one day. Instead, here are some logical combinations of steps that make for a nice training day.

Participant pre-work:

1. Read the introduction, Step 1, and Step 2 in *10 Steps to Be a Successful Manager.*

2. Meet with your team members to discuss their expectations of you. (Use tool 1.1 as a guide or starting point for choosing the questions to ask your staff.)

3. Bring a list of your current projects or key goals to the training session.

120 minutes—What does it mean to be a manager at *[your company name]*?

◆ Ask a senior manager to come in and share her or his vision of the contributions that managers can and ought to make. This section is intended to inspire the participating managers, to excite them about the potential of their work, and perhaps to make them feel a bit of pressure for how critical a role they perform. You might want to create a definition of managerial excellence like the sample I offer in Step 6.

◆ Ask participants, in small groups, to create a management filter based on the definition of excellence that the senior leader shared. Toward the end of this section of training, bring the leader back to hear each team present its filters. Encourage a lively discussion between the senior manager and participants about how to live the vision every day through actions, choices, and relationships. Also, ask participants to discuss any expectations from team members that seem to contradict those shared by the senior manager, ways of dealing with conflicting expectations, and how commonly these types of contradictions occur.

120 minutes—Step 1: Clarify, Negotiate, and Commit to Your Role

◆ Introduce the topic with a brief discussion of the key points and the participant's perspectives—encourage all points of view.

◆ The first activity of the day started participants thinking about managerial expectations from the senior managers' perspectives (they'll still need to circle back and have a one-on-one meeting with their managers). Have them define expectations in peer groups and then add those elements to their management filters. (You'll refine the filter as the day goes along, so have lots of blank copies on hand.) This may take about 45 minutes.

◆ Ask each participant to identify three ways in which his or her management needs to change over the next year to meet or exceed expectations. Allow 15 minutes for the work, then ask every manager to share his or her conclusions. If participants don't think changes are needed, here's a quote from the *10 Steps* Introduction that might help: "*Management A* produces *Results A.* If you want *Results B,* you can't get there using *Management A.* Great managers periodically tune up and align their practices and approaches to produce desired results."

100 minutes—Step 2: Understand Your Expected Results

◆ Introduce the topic with a brief discussion of the key points and the participants' perspectives—encourage all points of view.

◆ Form small groups of four or five managers. Have participants define grand-slam home run goals for their top three projects or goals. Allow 20 minutes for individual work, and then ask each manager to share her or his grand-slam goals. Have them get input and ideas from peers and others in their small groups. This sharing process may take up to 60 minutes, but it's time well spent if they're providing each other with great input. Process the exercise with lots of questions about why setting grand-slam goals is beneficial and why sharing them is even better.

20 minutes—Conclusion. Summarize the key learning points from the day. Encourage the managers to

◆ continue refining and using their management filters

- schedule a meeting to clarify expectations with their managers

- share their grand-slam home run goals with their managers and team members, and continue to refine those goals with their input.

Finally, talk about and agree on next steps that managers will take. Conclude the session.

Sample Agenda for a Two-Day Training

If possible, separate the two training days by a few days or a week so you can assign homework. (I love homework!)

Day 1

Use the pre-work and agenda presented for the one-day training. That's a logical first day of training whether you have one day, two days, or a week.

Participant homework:

1. Before training day 2, have the expectations meeting with your manager, and share your grand-slam goals with your manager and team members.

2. Fine-tune your management filter and list of grand-slam goals. Be prepared to share these at the beginning of day 2.

3. Ask each of your team members to identify the top three barriers that keep them from doing their best work. Add to that list the top three barriers in your way.

4. Read Steps 7 and 8 in *10 Steps to Be a Successful Manager*.

Day 2

60 minutes—Process the homework. Ask participants to tell how their meetings went and how they revised their filters and grand-slam goals.

150 minutes—Step 8: Obliterate Barriers

◆   Introduce the topic with a brief discussion of the key points and the participants' perspectives—encourage all points of view.

◆   Participants should have brought their list of the top barriers they and their team members face. Put participants into small groups and have each group identify the five most commonly mentioned barriers. For each of those five barriers, ask the group members to devise five potential strategies they could use to reduce or eliminate the barrier. Have each group present its list of five barriers and its 25 strategies. Notice the similarities. Ask the managers what should be done about these barriers. Offer to invite a senior manager in to hear their presentations (this would be great!). Have them decide what to do with the information they've put together, beyond the training session. This is real-world stuff, so follow-up is needed. The exercise may take up to 90 minutes.

◆ The second activity involves peer collaboration. Each participant should select and mention two barriers that were not discussed in the first activity For five minutes, the participant should collect from others in the group some ideas for how to obliterate the obstacle. Each person needs to take the full five minutes for this—you want them to stretch and generate lots of ideas.

130 minutes—Step 7: Plan the Work and Work the Plan—Flexibly

◆ Introduce the topic with a brief discussion of the key points and the participants' perspectives—encourage all points of view.

◆ Have participants complete weekly and daily plans based on worksheets 7.1 and 7.2 in *10 Steps.* Encourage them to include items from the barrier obliteration exercise, asking questions of their peers and sharing their rough ideas. Allow 25–30 minutes for this work.

◆ Once the daily and weekly plans are complete, group the participants into teams of peers who work together in some way. Have them do a 15-minute standing huddle in which they quickly share their weekly and daily plans with each other. Following the individual sharing, they may ask their peers clarifying questions. Process the exercise by asking what they learned and how the huddle format worked. Suggest they continue the peer huddles (and team huddles) back on the job.

20 minutes—Conclusion. Summarize the key learning points from the day. Encourage the managers to

◆ try the weekly and daily planning process for two weeks

◆ begin each day with a hit-list for barrier obliteration.

Talk about and agree on next steps to be taken. Conclude the session.

Sample Agenda for a One-Week (Five-Day) Training

If possible, schedule each day of the training one week apart so the training spans five weeks. This will allow for *lots* of homework. I know you might want to do the five days in one week, but that's not the more effective plan. The learning happens in the homework and application, and attending five days of training in a row is too much—people's brains will be fried and full by the end of day 2.

Day 1

Use the pre-work and agenda presented above for the one-day program.

After day 1, assign the homework described above for the first day of the two-day training program.

Day 2

Use the agenda presented above for day 2 of the two-day training.

Participant homework:

1. Read Steps 3 and 6 in *10 Steps to Be a Successful Manager*.

2. Write a first draft describing how you believe team member excellence looks for your department.

3. Make a list of current department metrics.

4. Do daily and weekly planning.

Day 3

60 minutes—Process the homework. Ask participants to share how their planning went. Ask for key learnings, aha moments, or questions on topics that have already been discussed. Give this some time. Don't rush into the new content until you've given people a chance to share their application experiences.

150 minutes—Step 3: Know Your Piece of the Business

◆ Introduce the topic with a brief discussion of the key points and the participants' perspectives—encourage all points of view.

◆ Ask a member of senior management to address the group about how the business measures success and performance. He or she should describe the three to six key metrics he or she looks at regularly to determine how well financial and performance goals are being met. He or she also should share the key red flags that suggest something may be wrong. Finally, ask the senior manager to offer advice for how participants should be measuring department performance. Encourage the group to ask questions and get into a meaty discussion about how the business is measured. Allow as much as 60 minutes for this discussion.

◆ Ask participants to describe in writing the two most important metrics that tell them how well their function is performing. Then ask them to share these two metrics in a small group of peers. Instruct the peers to ask questions or challenge the metrics if they don't seem like the right ones. Encourage people to disagree in order to help each other discover the right metrics. Allow 10 minutes of discussion for each person's metrics (more if needed). Ask people to share what they learned. This activity may take up to 60 minutes.

120 minutes—Step 6: Define and Model Excellence

◆ Introduce the topic with a brief discussion of the key points and the participants' perspectives—encourage all points of view.

◆ Have participants complete or fine-tune their definitions of excellence for their teams, using worksheet 6.1 from the book. Give them 20 minutes to work; then ask each manager to stand and read her or his definition of excellence. Ask the group to give feedback on whether it sounds like excellence. Allow 60 minutes for the readings with input.

◆ Ask participants to review table 6.1 from the book and then take 10 minutes to create their own list of potential conflicting behaviors to guard against. This is a list of three to five actions that would do the greatest damage by contradicting their definitions of excellence. This is their "must-not-do" cheat sheet. Ask a few people to read theirs to the group.

20 minutes—Conclusion. Summarize the key learning points from the day. Encourage the managers to

◆ share their definitions of excellence with their teams

◆ begin or continue tracking department metrics.

Talk about and agree on next steps to be taken. Assign homework. Conclude the session.

Participant homework:

1. Read Steps 4 and 5 in *10 Steps*.

2. Bring a job description for a position that is open in your department or will be open in the next month. Make and bring five copies of the job description. If you don't have an open position, don't worry about this part.

3. Share your definition of excellence with your team and get their input, ideas, and reactions.

Day 4

60 minutes—Process the homework. Ask participants to share how their teams responded to their definitions of excellence. Ask for key learnings, aha moments, or questions on topics that have already been discussed. Give this some time. Don't rush into the new content until you've given people a chance to share their application experiences.

150 minutes—Step 4: Build a Great Team

◆ Introduce the topic with a brief discussion of the key points and the participants' perspectives—encourage all points of view.

◆ Step 4 offers suggestions for creating strong teams: create connections, enliven minds, cultivate productive irreverence, and reinforce collaboration. Ask small teams of participants to create an organizational report card rating those four areas. They should grade the current culture, identify at least three reasons why they are assigning specific grades, and devise four strategies for improving each indicator. Have the teams share their report cards. Notice the similarities and differences. Ask the managers what ought to be done with this information. Because these are real data and managers are the ones to establish and reinforce the culture, the solutions lie with them. Encourage them to create a workable plan of action and make decisions or make things happen (booking of follow-up meetings, senior management review, and so forth) before the training session concludes today. Allow 120 minutes for this section.

120 minutes—Step 5: Choose Employees Wisely

◆ Introduce the topic with a brief discussion of the key points and the participants' perspectives—encourage all points of view.

◆ Some managers will have brought copies of job descriptions for open positions. Put the participants into groups of four. Assign each group one real job opening for this exercise.

If you have more job openings than small groups, ask for the right number of job descriptions from volunteers. Ask each group to create (1) criteria for job fit; (2) a meaty list of interview questions for their position, designed to determine candidate fit; and (3) an interview design process that will produce the best results. Invite someone from HR to roam the groups as a support person and to provide ideas and suggestions as needed. Give each team 60 minutes to do this work (more, if needed); then have each team share its work and what they learned from the process (allow another 45 minutes for sharing).

20 minutes—Conclusion. Summarize the key learning points from the day. Encourage the managers to

◆ follow up on the action items for building strong teams

◆ use the work they did on defining fit and interview questions as they move to fill the openings, and engage their peers in similar discussion for future openings.

Talk about and agree on next steps to be taken. Assign homework and conclude the session.

Participant homework:

1. Read Step 10 in *10 Steps to Be a Successful Manager.*

2. Complete some of the action items from the strong teams exercise.

3. If you have positions open, use the job-fit criteria and interview questions to make your candidate selections.

Day 5

60 minutes—Process the homework. Ask participants to share how the strong teams action plan is going. Ask managers who have interviewed candidates if they used the questions generated in the training and how that went. Ask for key learnings, aha moments, or questions on topics that have already been discussed. Give this some time. Don't rush into the new content until you've given people a chance to share their application experiences.

120 minutes—Step 10: Leave a Legacy of Capacity to Produce

◆ Introduce the topic with a brief discussion of the key points and the participants' perspectives—encourage all points of view.

◆ Have participants describe their personal visions for the legacy they want to leave as managers. Encourage them to work together or ask for input and help each other polish and practice their visions. Allow 45 minutes for them to work. If they finish early, encourage them to share with others who are done, and to continue refining and polishing their visions. Ask each participant to stand at the front of the room and share the legacy they wish to leave. This may take another 45 minutes.

◆ Ask participants to take 10 minutes to define three ways that they can begin to "be" their legacy today—ways of being that would align with their legacy vision. They should then share their three ways with the members of their small groups. Allow 15 minutes total.

60 minutes—Conclusion. Summarize the key learning points from the day and from the entire five days of training. Ask each manager to tell the class which parts of the training have been most helpful in honing his or her management craft. Ask the managers, in small groups, to create their own suggestions for what should come next to keep the development and reinforcement strong. Each team should share its suggestions with the whole class. Try to make some decisions about next steps if their ideas lend themselves to that. Conclude the program, and thank them for their generosity and participation

Reproducible Forms

This chapter presents full-size, reproducible versions of each example, table, tool, and worksheet used in *10 Steps to Be a Successful Manager*. Here's a list of what's included:

◆ Example 1.1: Management Filter: Basic Management Expectations

◆ Example 2.1: Sample Grand-Slam Home Run Goals

◆ Example 5.1: Sample Behavioral Questions for a Management Position Interview

◆ Table 6.1: Common Inconsistencies between What Managers Say Is Excellence and What Their Actions Communicate

◆ Table 8.1: Conditions Ripe for Practicing Barrier Obliteration

- Tool 1.1: Questions to Discover What People Expect from You

- Tool 4.1: Ways to Enliven Minds at Work

- Tool 4.2: Ways to Produce and Reinforce Collaboration

- Tool 5.1: Reference Check Questions and Why You Should Ask Them

- Tool 9.1: Typical Transition Behaviors

- Worksheet 1.1: The Management Filter

- Worksheet 3.1: Determining Metrics

- Worksheet 6.1: Defining Excellence

- Worksheet 7.1: Weekly Planning Checklist

- Worksheet 7.2: Daily Planning Checklist

- Worksheet 7.3: Daily Team Planning Checklist

- Worksheet 10.1: Creating Your Legacy Vision

EXAMPLE 1.1

Management Filter: Basic Management Expectations

Expectation	Filter Question: To what degree does taking this action or making this decision . . .	Level of Support for This Expectation		
Accountability and ownership	demonstrate my ownership and acknowledge the results for which I am accountable?	LOW	MEDIUM	HIGH
Make a positive contribution	make a positive difference to the business, the work culture, or my function?	LOW	MEDIUM	HIGH
Role model	present a positive and professional image of which I and the company can be proud?	LOW	MEDIUM	HIGH
Results orientation	demonstrate my focus and attention on producing results?	LOW	MEDIUM	HIGH
Master conversationalist and relationship builder	build the quality of dialogue and build productive relationships?	LOW	MEDIUM	HIGH
Focus on great management	show my commitment and dedication to solid management of my function and team?	LOW	MEDIUM	HIGH
Focus on accomplishment and organizational capacity	help build our results, and build the team's and the organization's capacity to deliver results in the future? To what degree does doing this make things better for today and tomorrow?	LOW	MEDIUM	HIGH
Inclusive and responsive	benefit from the ideas, concerns, and input of others? To what degree am I showing that I care about and will consider other perspectives and points of view?	LOW	MEDIUM	HIGH
Well-executed moments of leadership	demonstrate leadership? Am I stepping up to make a significant difference?	LOW	MEDIUM	HIGH

EXAMPLE 2.1

Sample Grand-Slam Home Run Goals

Goal	What a Grand Slam Looks Like	Why This Is a Grand Slam
Implement new booking engine by end of second quarter, within budget	Booking engine is implemented and welcomed by the staff. We've created contingency plans and ensured everyone is trained and feels comfortable with the new system before the switch is flipped. We've used this opportunity to train back-up staff. We've created positive momentum and excitement for the change that will fuel and support the next phases of booking development.	We're making a major change while reducing risk and increasing people's comfort and competence with the new system. We're taking the time and initiative to get people involved and active with the new system. We're building the team's energy for and ability to transition.
Cross-train staff by end of year, without going over budget	We use the cross-training as a way to better get to know people's strengths and career goals. Create a cross-training plan that builds collaboration and cooperation among people in different jobs. Build a plan that can account for absences and vacations so that the cross-training doesn't get set aside if someone is away. Cross-train at least two people for each position.	The plan is robust and more likely to be implemented as intended. Most cross-training plans get set aside because they don't account for changes. The plan also reinforces our need to create better relationships and understand people's strengths and career interests.
Develop and implement a product development review process by July 31	Take the time to talk to key stakeholders before creating the process. Create a process that will be widely supported by key stakeholders, one that respects everyone's precious time. The process should include practices that continue the review in the event that some participants are out of town. The process ought to be inclusive while not getting out of hand in terms of the number of people sitting in meetings. Create a process to ensure that product managers collect and communicate key analyses and metrics before the review meetings occur.	Creating the project with these considerations will ensure that people are prepared to participate and that decisions can be made in a timely manner. This approach also will support our goals to use time wisely and be inclusive.

EXAMPLE 5.1

Sample Behavioral Questions for a
Management Position Interview

1. Each member of a leadership team brings unique strengths and weaknesses. For the last/current leadership team you belonged to,
   a. describe the team—its size, members.
   b. describe the unique skills and talents that you brought to the team *beyond* your functional knowledge.
   c. describe the ways in which you relied on other team members for coaching and advice.

2. What do you think are the ideal composition and function of a leadership team? How often should it meet? What should the focus of its meetings be? How else should members work together? What authority/ownership should members assert with each other?

3. Describe a time when you asserted yourself at a regular leadership team meeting. What was the situation? What did you say? What were the results?

4. Describe the two contributions you made in the last year that you are most proud of? How have these contributions helped the company?

5. Beyond your functional projects and tasks, in what ways have you helped the company improve its ability to manage, execute, and react to change?

6. Tell me about a peer with whom you have had the most difficulty working? What made it difficult? What did you do about it? What were the results?

7. If we were to ask your current/last peers and manager to describe the greatest strengths you brought to the company, what do you think they would say? Why?

8. Over the next two years, how would you like to grow as a leader? How will you approach getting this development?

9. Over the last year, what was the largest problem you had to solve? How did you approach it? What did you do? What were the results?

10. Describe your leadership and management style. How do you ensure everyone on your team is working on the right stuff? How do you communicate? What's your belief about what makes people perform their best?

11. As a member of the leadership team, the *[open position title]* needs to communicate fully but appropriately with his or her teams, peers, and managers. How would you approach that responsibility? What, if anything, should be off-limits? What do team members need to know, and what do peers and managers need to know?

TABLE 6.1

Common Inconsistencies between What Managers Say Is Excellence and What Their Actions Communicate

What They Say	But What They Do
They value candor and diversity.	They become defensive when challenged or when people offer alternative ideas.
They want meetings to be productive and move work forward.	They facilitate ineffective meetings and book meetings that aren't viewed as a good use of time.
They value collaboration and teamwork.	They reward and reinforce only or primarily individual contributions.
They expect all employees to model the highest standards of professionalism.	They gossip and denigrate peer managers in front of team members.
They want the team to be change resilient and agile.	They resist changes that make them personally uncomfortable or require a lot of work.
They want the team to be customer focused and to provide excellent internal and external service.	They neglect to collect and/or listen to customer feedback or measure the team's performance based on customer-centric metrics.
They want the team to think creatively and generate ideas for improvement.	They don't support team members who want to get together to share and discuss ideas.

TABLE 8.1

Conditions Ripe for Practicing Barrier Obliteration

When	What to Look For
Team meetings	Notice energy-level drops and nonverbal communication. If people seem frustrated or concerned, they may be dealing with mucky muck.
Your staff meetings with peers	Notice the people or topics that provoke resistance. What's going on and how might you help?
Project reviews	Notice the constraints and steps along the process that are slow or stalled. Which process steps cause the most delay and frustration?
Requests you need to repeat	If you make a request and the person does not complete the request, he or she is likely dealing with some kind of barrier.
Things that make your eyes roll	Pay attention to your own body language. Instead of putting up with frustration and red tape again and again, fix it!
Water-cooler complaints	Listen to what people are talking about. Their complaints often are caused by mucky muck.

TOOL 1.1

Questions to Discover What People Expect from You

Topic Area	Questions to Determine Expectations
Basic job function	• How do you define quality of work? • What are your expectations regarding deadlines and communication of work status? • What does "being prepared" mean?
Decision making	• What is your expectation of me regarding making and communicating decisions? • What types of decisions would you like me to include you in making?
Work environment	• How would you describe the work environment you expect me to build and reinforce? • In what ways would you like to see the company's culture change? • What role do you believe I should play in creating that transformation? • Is there anything about the department's current culture that you think ought to change or improve?
Creativity and innovation	• What does it mean to "be creative"? • How important are creativity and innovation, and what are your expectations of me regarding them? • In what ways would you like me and my group to generate new ideas and improve results?
Team development and productivity	• Will you describe for me your vision of how a well-functioning team looks and feels? • What expectations do you have regarding team development and productivity? • What are your expectations regarding the way I will manage and correct poor performance? • How much time do you think I ought to spend coaching others?
Communication	• What does "effective communication" look like to you? • What are your expectations of me regarding communication? • What do you expect of me regarding attending and conducting meetings?
Growth and development	• Everyone needs to continue to grow. In what two ways would you most like to see me grow and develop over the next year?
Results orientation	• What does it mean to be "results oriented"? • What are your expectations of me regarding getting results and being results oriented?
Partnership	• How important are partnership and collaboration? • What are your expectations of me regarding our level of partnership and collaboration? • In what ways would you like to see partnership and collaboration improve?
Ethics and role modeling	• What does it mean to "represent the company well"? • What are your expectations for how managers will conduct themselves and represent the company?

TOOL 4.1

Ways to Enliven Minds at Work

Focus Area	Enlivening Technique
Connection to the company	Be as transparent with company information as you possibly can. Keep your team informed. Share their feedback with peers and your manager so they feel their voices have been heard.
Energy	Have quick and energetic huddles instead of meetings. Be energetic yourself. Encourage people to get up and move around throughout the day. Hire high-energy people. Help team members manage stress, and make sure no one is working too many hours on a consistent basis.
Participation in team conversations	Ask provocative and evocative questions. Elicit everyone's input and show your gratitude for ideas, even contrary ones. Ask people to comment on topics that you know interest them. Send out questions before meetings so people can prepare their thoughts.
Collaboration	Ask for team or subteam recommendations. Put people into pairs and small groups to work on projects. Acknowledge and reinforce group accomplishment.

TOOL 4.2

Ways to Produce and Reinforce Collaboration

Factor	Ideas for Producing and Reinforcing Collaboration
Physical location	House teams together or in a way that encourages informal conversation. Make sure that informal meeting spaces are available. If the team is located in more than one place, get members together on a regular basis and encourage them to use technology to have both informal and planned conversations. Give them unrestricted access to phone, email, Internet phone, teleconferencing services, and web seminar software.
Communication processes	Make it a habit to use a portion of your team meetings for collaboration. When people come to your office with questions or ideas, encourage them to gather a few peers to talk through the issue (eventually, they'll do this before coming to you—a beautiful thing).
Tasks and assignments	Assign projects and tasks to teams, subteams, and pairs of peers. Get your team in the habit of working together.
Goals and measurements	Make sure that at least half of your employees' goals are team, subteam, or pair goals. Use team measures along with individual measures for any evaluations, pay raise considerations, promotions, and bonuses. (I don't recommend linking evaluations to pay raises.)
Workplace culture	Reinforce and show appreciation for collaborative work. Model collaboration by asking team members and peers to work with you on your tasks and projects. Encourage diverse opinions and points of view. Show support when team members get together for informal conversations or meetings.

TOOL 5.1

Reference Check Questions and Why You Should Ask Them

Question	Why Ask This Question
How did you know this person? On what types of projects did you work together?	To better understand their professional relationship and get a feel for how well the reference remembers the candidate.
Tell me about [candidate name]'s job. What did he or she do while at [company name]?	To get a feel for how well the canddate's description of the job matches what the reference remembers.
Everyone has special talents—things they do better than others. What did [candidate name] do better than most people at the company?	This will give you a feel for the candidate's greatest strengths. That's important because those strengths will be the key attributes that you'll be buying if you hire the person. Are these the strengths you most need right now?
We all get stressed every now and then. What tended to stress out [candidate name]?	This is a way of asking about weaknesses and of learning what type of environment will set the candidate off. It's a critical question to determine fit.
We obviously think highly of [candidate name]. If we extend an offer and if the offer is accepted, what would your advice be to [candidate name]'s new manager for how to get the best performance from [candidate name]?	I love this question. Believe it or not, most references, even the close buddies, are totally honest here. This is where you learn what kind of management a candidate will require and whether the candidate leans toward independence or dependence, high or low maintenance. These are important fit issues.
If you had another position open, would you hire [candidate name] again? Why/why not?	The reference likely will say "yes," but notice whether and for how long he or she hesitates. If the "yes" is immediate, that's great. If it takes a while or if the "yes" is qualified with a statement like, "Well, my company doesn't do that kind of work anymore," that's not so good.
For management candidates: Aside from functional expertise, in what ways did [candidate name] add to the effectiveness of the leadership team?	This will tell you the candidate's contribution to the management team. If the reference offers nothing beyond the candidate's functional expertise (the reference will struggle to answer the question), take a pass on the applicant. You need someone who'll strengthen the team in many ways.
For management candidates: How did [candidate name] maximize team performance. How did she or he ensure the team was doing its best work?	The reference may struggle with this one, but it will likely give you some insight into the candidate's management style. If the reference says he or she doesn't know, that's likely not true and may be a red flag.

TOOL 9.1

Typical Transition Behaviors

Transition Phase	Behavior You May See
Phase 1: Ending	Avoidance, clinging to the old, going through the motions, disbelief, shock, anger, mistakes, sabotage, carelessness
Phase 2: Neutral zone	Detachment, withdrawal, confusion, lack of attentiveness, mood swings, indifference, creativity, risk taking, experimentation, participation
Phase 3: New beginning	Behavior consistent with the change, focus on purpose, renewed energy, clarity of role, feeling of competence

WORKSHEET 1.1

The Management Filter

Instructions: In the first column, list expectations (the results *you* are expected to produce, not what you expect of others). In column two, translate each expectation into a question. For example, if you're expected to build collaboration, column two might read, "To what degree does taking this action or making this decision increase team member collaboration?" You want to translate the expectation into a question that will help you determine how well your actions and decisions support the achievement of the expectation. When you have columns one and two filled in, you can use the filter. That is, you assess potential actions and decisions for alignment with expectations by assessing whether each one supports your intentions. Circle **LOW, MEDIUM,** or **HIGH** to indicate how well the action or decision supports your expectation. For example, if you want to improve collaboration and you have decided to begin weekly collaboration meetings, you would rate alignment as HIGH.

Expectation	Filter Question: To what degree does taking this action or making this decision. . .	Level of Support for This Expectation
		LOW MEDIUM HIGH
		LOW MEDIUM HIGH
		LOW MEDIUM HIGH
		LOW MEDIUM HIGH
		LOW MEDIUM HIGH
		LOW MEDIUM HIGH
		LOW MEDIUM HIGH
		LOW MEDIUM HIGH

LOW MEDIUM HIGH

LOW MEDIUM HIGH

LOW MEDIUM HIGH

LOW MEDIUM HIGH

LOW MEDIUM HIGH

LOW MEDIUM HIGH

LOW MEDIUM HIGH

LOW MEDIUM HIGH

LOW MEDIUM HIGH

LOW MEDIUM HIGH

LOW MEDIUM HIGH

LOW MEDIUM HIGH

LOW MEDIUM HIGH

WORKSHEET 3.1

Determining Metrics

Instructions: Answer these questions as a group at your next team meeting. Use the answers to help you narrow and focus your list of the metrics to track regularly.

1. Why does this team exist? In what ways is it expected to contribute to the company?

2. What are our current department metrics, and what is our current level of performance on these metrics?

3. Do these measures indicate how well our department is performing against the key areas to which the company expects us to contribute?

4. If we were to ask our key internal or external customers, would they think these metrics were most important? If not, what indicators would our customers advocate we measure?

5. Can we do well on these metrics and produce poor results? If so, why?

6. If we could look at only two indicators to determine the team's results, what would those two indicators be? What's the best way to measure those indicators? At what frequency should we measure and review them? Who should own the collecting and communicating of data? How are we performing against these metrics today—do we know?*

7. How should we move forward?

*If the answer is "no," get that done very rapidly and have another quick review meeting with the team.

WORKSHEET 6.1

Defining Excellence

Instructions: Describe performance excellence for each performance factor.

Performance Factor	How You Define Excellence for This Factor
Communication	
Collaboration	
Professionalism	
Creativity and innovation	
Project performance	
Meetings	
Problem identifying and solving	
Change and agility	
Results and performance	
Team and organization	

WORKSHEET 7.1

Weekly Planning Checklist

Instructions: Use this planning checklist to set aside time and energy for the most important work tasks. Start by defining a grand-slam home run goal for the week (an accomplishment that would make a significant positive impact on the department, project, and/or company). Write down two to four items for the other planning elements and then use this information to plan your week. Review and revise this worksheet daily or as needed.

Planning Element	Your Plan for the Week
Gland-slam home run for the week:	
Meetings and conversations I need to schedule	
Decisions needed, and by whom	
Coaching and developing for the week	
Any *must-not-miss* items	
Potential barriers to hitting the grand slam for the week	

WORKSHEET 7.2

Daily Planning Checklist

Instructions: Transfer your weekly grand-slam home run goal from the weekly planning worksheet. At the beginning of each day, take 10 minutes to define the actions you intend to take for each planning element. Carry this checklist with you to meetings and review it midday to ensure you're on track and focused on the right work.

Planning Element	Your Plan for the Day
Gland-slam home run for the week (transfer from weekly checklist):	
Two or three actions I can take today that will make the greatest difference	
Team focus—any adjustments to be made	
Barriers I need to obliterate	
Meetings and preparation needed	

WORKSHEET 7.3

Daily Team Planning Checklist

Instructions: Write the names of your team members in the left-hand column. Ask each team member to share his or her top two priorities for the day at a morning huddle or informal check-in. Write the priorities in the right-hand column. Refer to this checklist during meetings and informal conversations throughout the day.

Team Member	Top Two Priorities for the Day